"In the name of Allah,
the Compassionate, the Merciful"

3rd Edition
Baltimore, Maryland, USA
www.ad-duha.org
support@ad-duha.org

Ad-Duha's mission is to help Muslim families provide their children with quality Islamic materials. Therefore, we ask that our customers help us in this task by honoring the copyright (i.e. not making copies or posting online) of our products.

This copyright is intended to ensure that the school can stay financially viable (i.e. cover the costs of development, production, and marketing) through the legitimate sale of its products. Honoring the rights of everyone, including those of your Muslim brothers/sisters, is sacred in Islaam.

If you would like to learn more about copyright law in Islaam, please visit our web site (click on "Terms of Use" at the bottom of any page) for a comprehensive summary of the Fatwa (religious ruling issued by scholars) regarding this matter.

ISBN 978-1438259086

Printed in the United States of America

How to Use These Books

The Mini Tafseer Book Series is designed to teach children the Tafseer (exegesis) of all the suwaar (chapters) in the 30th Part of the Qur'aan. Each book in this 38 book series covers a different surah. The books feature:

- Special facts about the surah
- Arabic text of the surah
- English transliteration (to assist non-Arabic speakers)
- English translation
- Simplified Tafseer
- Illustrations/Coloring pages (no animals/humans)
- Highlighted Arabic vocabulary
- Sahih Ahadith
- One sentence summary of what the surah is about
- Review section
- Notes on the text (additional facts and information)

Teaching Tips:

If your younger child has trouble going through the whole book in one sitting, or does not retain all of the information taught, then just focus on the Tafseer pages first (i.e. those that explain the verses of the surah) and save the additional information contained in the Quick Facts, What's Special, Asbaab An-Noozool, and Vocabulary sections* for later when your child has mastered the Tafseer.

For older or advanced students who need more of a challenge, you can take time to go through all sections and discuss the lesson notes for that section (located at the end of the text). This will make lessons more challenging and provide a deeper understanding of the Tafseer, and Allah knows best.

**Some books may not contain all of these sections.*

Mini Tafseer Book Series

Suratul-Faatiha

Quick Facts about Suratul-Faatiha...

Suratul-Faatiha was **revealed in Makkah** before the Hijrah to Madinah.[1] (Makkah is the city where Rasulullah ﷺ was born, where the Kaabah is located, and where Rasulullah ﷺ first taught Islaam.)

Suratul-Faatiha has **seven verses**.[2]

There are so many great things about Suratul-Faatiha that we cannot fit them all on this page! You will have to read the book to learn more about this **precious jewel of the Qur'aan.**

So what is Suratul-Faatiha all about?

It is about asking Allah for help.
Allah will help us by **giving us two things** we want, and **protecting us from two things** we don't want because He loves us.

Now let's learn what makes Suratul-Faatiha so…

The **first** thing that is **so special** about Suratul-Faatiha is that it was the…

First Complete Surah!

When Rasulullahﷺ started to receive revelation from Allah, it was usually only a few ayaat (verses) at a time, not a whole surah.

But when Allah sent Suratul-Faatiha, He sent it complete with **all seven ayaat at one time**.

That means Suratul-Faatiha was the **first complete surah** revealed to Rasulullahﷺ.

1st

The **second** thing that is **so special** about Suratul-Faatiha is that it is...

One of Two Lights from Allah

Ibn 'Abbaas رضي الله عنه said, "While Angel Gibreel was with the Messenger of Allah ﷺ, he heard a noise from above. Gibreel lifted his sight to the sky and said, 'This is a door in heaven being opened, and it has never been opened before now.' An angel descended from that door and came to the Prophet ﷺ and said, 'Receive the glad tidings of ***two lights*** *that you have been given, which no other prophet before you was given:* ***The Opening of the Book (Suratul-Faatiha)*** *and the last ayaat*[3] *of Suratul-Baqarah. You will not read a letter of them, but will gain its benefit.'"*

(Sahih Muslim and An-Nasa'i)

The **third** thing that is **so special** about Suratul-Faatiha is that it is...

The Greatest Surah in the Qur'aan!

Ubayy bin Ka`b ﵁ reported that Rasulullah ﷺ said, "I will teach you the ***greatest Surah in the Qur'an*** *before you leave the Masjid." He (the prophet) held my hand and when he was about to leave the Masjid, I said, "O Messenger of Allah ﷺ! You said, 'I will teach you the greatest Surah in the Qur'an.' He said, "Yes. It is the* ***seven repeated (verses)*** *(i.e. Suratul-Faatiha) and the Glorious Qur'an that I was given."'*

(Sahih Al-Bukhari, Abu Dawud, An-Nasaa'i, and Ibn Majah)

I will teach you the greatest surah in the Qur'aan...
It is the seven repeated...

The **fourth** thing that is **so special** about Suratul-Faatiha is that it has...

Seven Names

You can remember that it has **seven names** because it also has **seven verses**.

Suratul-Faatiha's names are[4]...

1) **Umm Al-Ki-taab** (Mother of the Book)
2) **Umm Al-Qur'aan** (Mother of the Qur'aan)
3) **Sab'a Ma-thaa-neey** (Seven Repeated Verses)
4) **As-Sa-laah** (The Prayer)
5) **Al-Hamd** (The Praise)
6) **Ar-Rooq-yah** (The Cure for Evil Eye)
7) **Ash-Shi-faa'** (The Cure for Illness)

See the *Bonus Section* at the end of this book to learn more about what each of these names means.

The **fifth** and **most important** thing that is so special about Suratul-Faatiha is...

Allah answers every ayah we say!

Suratul-Faatiha has **two parts**,
one for us to say, and the other for
Allah to say.[5]

AND that is not all...

Allah promises that we will get
everything we ask for in this surah.[6]
Allah must love us very much.

How much do you...

...love Allah?

Now let's get ready to learn more about Suratul-Faatiha...

We will start by learning **4 new words** from the Qur'aan. These are words that are used in Suratul-Faatiha and in many other suwaar (that word is the plural of surah) that you will study as well.

The more words you know from the Qur'aan, the better you will understand each surah that you learn insha-Allah.

Understanding the Qur'aan is what Allah wants us to do.

So let's get started right now!

4 NEW WORDS

Vocabulary List

Keep a look out for the following vocabulary words while you read. These words will help you remember the meaning of Suratul-Faatiha, insha-Allah.

the praise	ٱلْحَمْدُ (al-hamd)
The Merciful	ٱلرَّحِيمِ (ar-ra-heem)
people Allah is angry with	ٱلْمَغْضُوبِ (al-mag-doob)
people who go away from the right path	ٱلضَّآلِّينَ (ad-daa-leen)

Now that we are ready, we need to start the right way...

You see, Allah and Rasulullah ﷺ have taught us the **right way** to do everything, even the right way to start reciting from the Qur'aan.

There are **two things** we should say before we start reading a surah from the Qur'aan, and you will learn about these two things right now...

#1 We say the Isti'aathah[7]...

I seek refuge with Allah from the
cursed Shaytaan.

('A-'oo-thoo-bil-laa-he-me-nash-shay-taa-nir-ra-jeem)

أَعُوذُ بِٱللَّهِ مِنَ

ٱلشَّيْطَانِ ٱلرَّجِيمِ

We start reading Qur'aan by asking Allah to protect us from Shaytaan and...

#2 We say the Basmallah[8]...

In the name of Allah, the Entirely Merciful,
the Especially Merciful.

(Bis-mil-laa-hir-rah-maa-nir-ra-heem)

We remember Allah and say how great He is for giving us so many wonderful blessings.

Okay!

We are ready to go now! You know your **new words** and you've said the **Isti'aathah** and **Basmallah**...

Now it is time to learn what we say in Suratul-Faatiha...

...and what Allah says back to us!

All praise is due to Allah, Lord of the Worlds,

(Al-ham-doo lil-laa-hee rab-bil 'aa-la-meen)

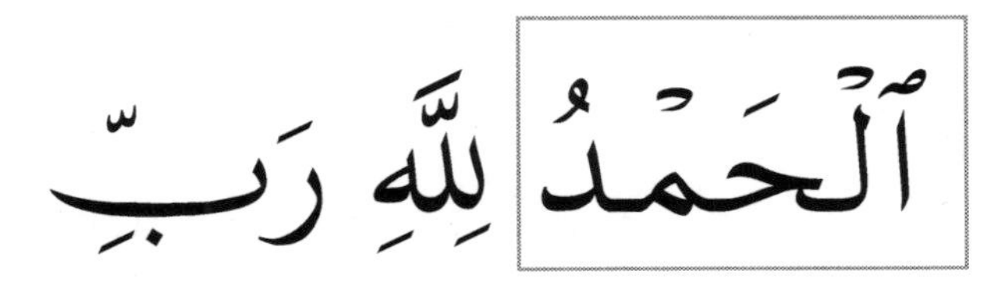

We say,

"Allah, You are the best. You are in charge of all the worlds."

Allah says,

"My servant has praised Me."

(That means we have said good things about Allah.)

The Entirely Merciful, the Especially Merciful:

(Ar-rah-maa-nir-ra-heem)

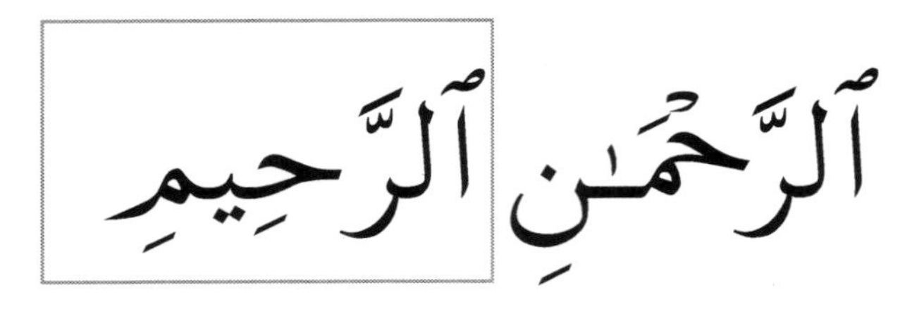

We say,

"You are the one who gives us everything we need and takes care of us."

Allah says,

"My servant has extolled Me."

(That means that we know Allah is the only one who gives us every blessing that we have.)

What are some of the blessings Allah has given you?

Draw a picture in the box!

Sovereign of the Day of Recompense,

(Maa-li-kee yow-mid-deen)

We say,

"Allah, You are King of the day when we will come back to you to be judged after we die."

Allah says,

"My servant has exalted Me."

(That means we have said how great Allah is!)

It is You we worship and You we ask for help.

(Eey-yaa-ka na'-boo-doo wa-eey-yaa-ka nas-ta-'een)

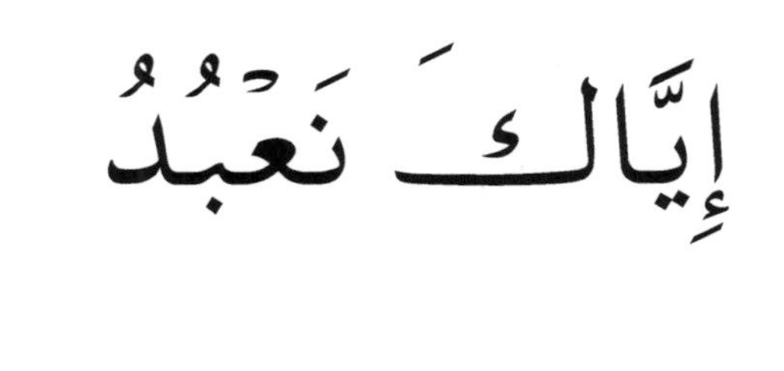

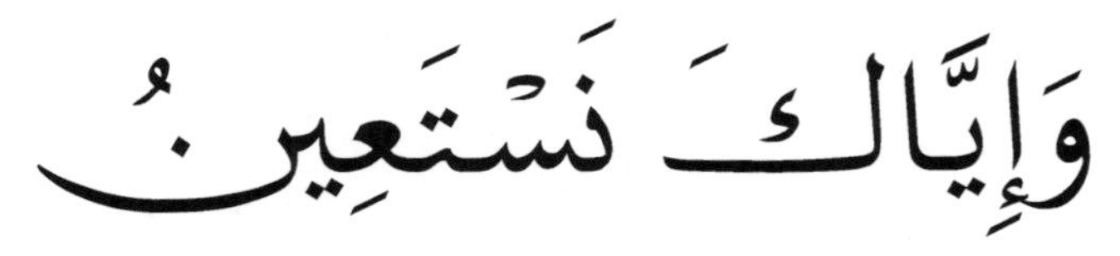

We say,

"Allah, You are the only one we pray to, and You are the only one we ask help from."

Allah says,

"This is between Me and My servant, and My servant will have what he has asked for."

Now that we have praised Allah, there are 2 things we ask Allah to give us in Suratul-Faatiha...

Guide us to the straight path,

(Ih-dee-nas-see-raa-tal moos-ta-qeem)

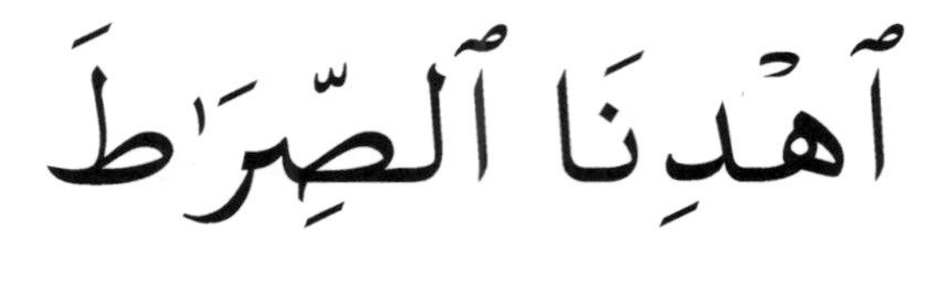

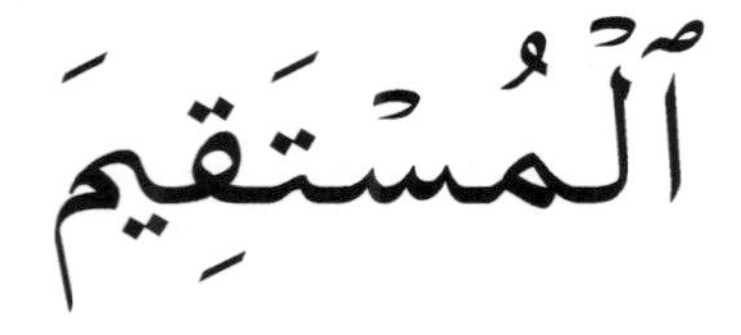

1

We ask Allah,

"Show us how to be good Muslims."

The path of those upon whom You have bestowed favor;

(Sir-aa-tal-la-thee-na an-‘am-ta ‘a-lay-him)

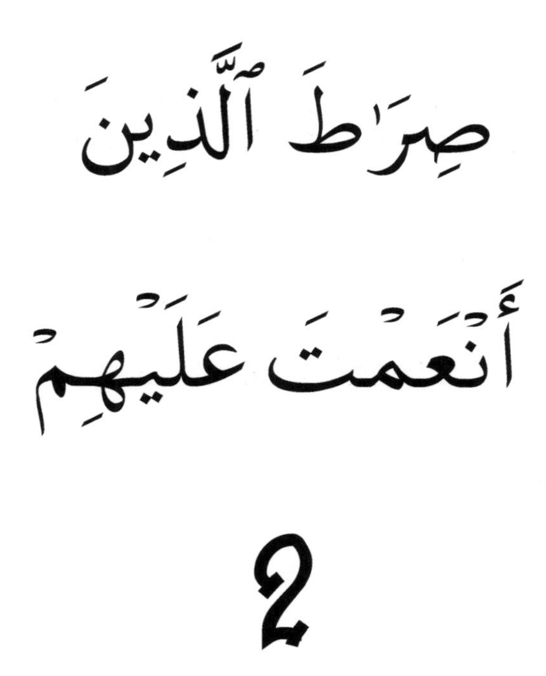

We ask Allah,

“Show us how to be among those You have blessed.”

Next, there are 2 things we ask Allah to protect us from in Suratul-Faatiha...

Not of those who have (evoked) Your anger,

(Ghay-ril magh-doo-bee alay-him)

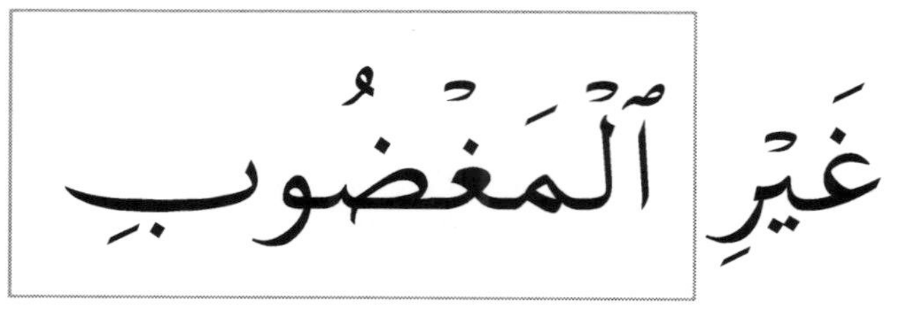

1

We ask Allah,

"**<u>Protect</u>** us from doing things that would make You angry with us."

Or of those who go astray.

(Wa-lad-daaal-leen)

2

We ask Allah,

"**Protect** us from going away from Islaam."

After we ask for our two gifts
and two protections...

Allah says,

"This is for My servant, and he will have what he has asked for."

See how much Allah loves us!

When we ask Allah for help, Allah will give us the **two good things** we ask for, and protect us from the **two bad things** we are afraid of...if we ask nicely Insha-Allah.

The End

Bonus Section

You learned in the beginning of this book that Suratul-Faatiha has **seven names**, now we will take a moment to explain what each of the names means...

Names 1 & 2

Umm Al-Kitaab & Umm Al-Qur'aan

Umm in Arabic means mother (something that begins or contains everything), and Kitaab means book.

So, Faatiha is the Mother of the Book (i.e. the Qur'aan) because it is the first surah (chapter) in the Qur'aan, and it talks about all of the important things that you learn about in the rest of the Qur'aan.[9]

Name 3

Sab'a Ma-thaa-neey

Sab'a in Arabic means seven, and Ma-thaa-neey means to say something many times.

Suratul-Faatiha has seven verses and we repeat these seven verses at least **17 times** a day in the five daily Salawaat (prayers). That's a lot! If you add all the Sunnah prayers before and after the Salaah, then we recite it at least **32 times** a day! [10]

Name 4

As-Sa-laah

Salah in Arabic means prayer,
like the five prayers we make each day.

We have to recite Suratul-Faatiha
in every rakah (unit) of every prayer,
every day.

If you do not say Suratul-Faatiha in every
rakah of every prayer, every day, your
Salaah is not complete. That is why
Suratul-Faatiha is called As-Salaah.[11]

Name 5

Al-Hamd

Hamd in Arabic means praise (to say something good about someone).

In Suratul-Faatiha Allah has taught us how to say the best things about Him, so that is why Faatiha is called Al-Hamd.

Names 6 & 7

Ar-Rooq-yah & Ash-Shi-faa'

Both Rooq-yah and Shi-faa' in Arabic mean to cure someone who is sick.

Rooq-yah means to cure a person who has been affected by the envy of someone else (Evil Eye)[12] and Shi-faa' is a cure for someone who has a sickness of their body, like a cold or sprained ankle.

Some of the Sahaaba (companions of Rasulullahﷺ) used to use Faatiha to cure people who were sick. When Rasulullahﷺ heard about this, he told the other Sahaaba that it is true, Faatiha can cure people.[13]

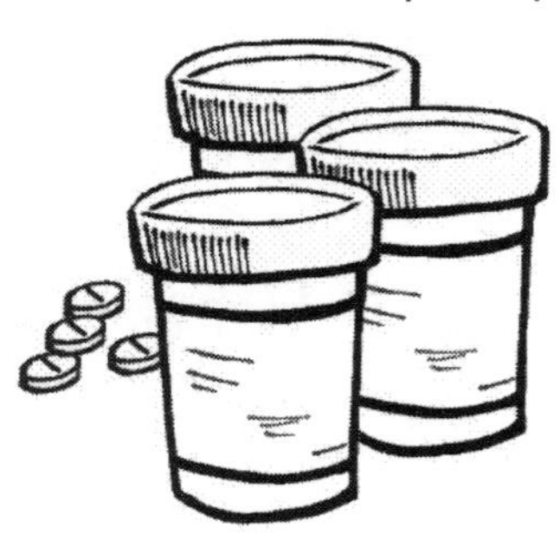

Suratul-Faatiha Review

What is Suratul-Faatiha about?

It is about asking Allah for help and how Allah will give us what we ask for because He loves us.

In what city was Suratul-Faatiha revealed?

Makkah

How many verses does Suratul-Faatiha have?

Seven

Is Suratul-Faatiha a light?

Yes, Allah gave Suratul-Faatiha as a light to Rasulullahﷺ and the Muslims.

Did Allah give something like Suratul-Faatiha to any people before us?

No

What is the Greatest Surah in the Qur'aan?

Suratul-Faatiha

How many names does Suratul-Faatiha have?

Suratul-Faatiha has seven names.

What are the seven names?

1) Umm Al-Ki-taab (Mother of the Book)

2) Umm Al-Qur'aan (Mother of the Qur'aan)

3) Sab'a Ma-thaa-neey (Seven oft repeated verses)

4) As-Sa-laah (The Prayer)

5) Al-Hamd (The Praise)

6) Ar-Rooq-yah (The Cure for the Evil Eye)

7) Ash-Shi-faa' (The Cure for illness)

Why is Suratul-Faatiha called Umm Al-Kitaab and Umm Al-Qur'aan?

Because Suratul-Faatiha is the first Surah and it talks about all the important things that are mentioned in the rest of the Qur'aan.

Why is Suratul-Faatiha called Sab'aa Ma-thaa-neey?

Suratul-Faatiha has seven verses and we read it from 17-32 times a day in our prayers.

Why is Suratul-Faatiha called As-Sa-laah?

Because you have to recite Suratul-Faatiha in each rakah, of every prayer, every day.

Why is Suratul-Faatiha called Al-Hamd?

Suratul-Faatiha teaches us how to praise Allah the right way.

Why is Suratul-Faatiha called Ar-Rooq-yah?

Suratul-Faatiha can be used to cure the Evil Eye.

Why is Suratul-Faatiha called Ash-Shi-faa'?

Suratul-Faatiha can be used to cure illnesses.

What is the <u>most important</u> thing, that makes Suratul-Faatiha so special?

Allah answers every verse that we say.

What are the two things we ask Allah to give us in Suratul-Faatiha?

Show us how to be good Muslims, and how to be among those Allah has blessed.

What are the two things that we ask Allah to protect us from in Suratul-Faatiha?

Keep us from being misguided and doing things that would make Allah angry with us.

Will Allah give us what we ask for?

Yes!

Notes to the text

[1]Al-Faatiha was revealed in Makkah as Ibn Abbaas, Qatadah and Abu Al-`Aliyah stated. Allah said,

﴿وَلَقَدْ ءاتَيْنَـكَ سَبْعًا مِّنَ الْمَثَانِي﴾

(And indeed, We have bestowed upon you the seven Mathani) (seven repeatedly recited verses). (Qur'aan15:87)
(Tafseer Ibn Kathir)

This verse (15:87) was revealed in Makkah before the Hijrah to Madinah, and it is referring to Suratul-Faatiha (i.e. the seven oft-repeated verses). Therefore Faatiha must have been revealed in Makkah before the revelation of this ayah.

As for the Hijrah, this is the name of the migration of the Muslims from Makkah, to the city of Yathrib (later called Madinah) in the northeast. The Hijrah took place after Rasulullahﷺ taught in Makkah for approximately 12-13 years. Rasulullahﷺ lived and taught in Madinah for ten years after the Hijrah until his death.

It must be noted, that although Faatiha is the first surah in the Qur'aan according to order, and it was the first complete surah (all verses revealed at the same time), it is not the first revelation that was received by Rasulullahﷺ. The first verses, or ayaat, of the Qur'aan to be revealed, were Suratul-Alaq, ayah 1-5 *"Read in the name of your Lord..."*

The order in which the Qur'aan was revealed was linked to specific events in time so that the people would understand the verses in context and could pass this information on to later generations. Once all the verses of the Qur'aan were revealed, Angel Gibreel read the entire Qur'aan, with the surahs in the order we know them today, from beginning to end with Rasulullahﷺ twice during Ramadaan in the year of Rasulullah'sﷺ death.

The Qur'aan we have today was written down based on this order, from the memories and written records of the Sahaaba, after the death of Rasulullahﷺ.

2 "*And indeed, We have bestowed upon you the seven Mathaani) (seven repeatedly recited verses), (i.e. Suratul-Faatiha).*"
(Qur'aan15:87)

"There is no disagreement over the view that Al-Faatiha contains seven ayaat. According to the majority of the recitors of Al-Kufah, a group of the Companions, the Tabi`een, and a number of scholars from the successive generations, the Bismillah is a separate ayah in its beginning."
(Tafseer Ibn Kathir)

[3] There is more than one opinion as to which ayaat this Hadith is referring to (although it is generally understood to mean v. 285-286), as the Hadith only mentions "the end" of Baqarah.

Based on other narrations on the benefits of Baqarah, this could mean the last two or the last three ayaat of the surah. There is support for both views from the Sahih ahadith (see below). So, one can teach the number of verses that they feel have the best evidence, and Allah knows best.

Abu Mas'ood al-Ansaari رضي الله عنه narrated that the Prophet ﷺ said, "*Whoever recites the last two verses of Suratul-Baqarah (v. 285-286) at night, they will suffice him (i.e. protect him from harm).*" *(Sahih Al-Bukhaari and Sahih Muslim)*

In another narration, Abu Bakr ibn Dawood رضي الله عنه said, "*I did not think that any sane person could sleep without reciting the last three verses of Suratul-Baqarah.*"
(Al-Nawawi graded this narration as Sahih according to the conditions of Al-Bukhaari and Muslim. This statement has also been attributed to Ali رضي الله عنه in a different narration.)

The Prophet ﷺ also said, "*Allah inscribed a book, two thousand years before He created the heavens and the earth, from which the last two verses of Suratul-Baqarah were revealed. If they*

are recited for three nights, no Shaytaan (devil) will remain in the house."
(Tirmidhi, and classed as Sahih by Al-Albaani)

Note: Another hadith often quoted as evidence to recite the last three ayaat of Suratul-Baqarah is weak and should not be used as evidence...

'Abdullah ibn Mas'ood ﵁ is narrated as saying, *"Whoever recites the following ten verses of Suratul-Baqarah at night, Shaytaan will not enter his house that night: the first four verses, the verse of al-Kursi and the two verses after it, and the last three verses."*

In other narrations, the following words are also added... *"No Shaytaan will approach him or his family that night, nor anything that he hates; and if recited to an insane person, that person will be cured."*

This is a very frequently quoted hadith, but it has a broken chain of transmission. Of course, there is no harm in reciting any or all of Suratul-Baqarah, but we should not recite these specific ten ayaat with the hope of attaining the rewards/benefits mentioned in the above weak narration. Rather, we can look to the rewards mentioned in the Sahih ahadith regarding the same ayaat that are mentioned above and in the books of ahadith, and Allah knows best.

4 Abu Hurayrah ﵁ said that the Messenger of Allah ﷺ said, *"Al-Hamdu lillahi Rabbil-`Aalamin is*

the Mother of the Qur'an, the Mother of the Book, and the seven repeated ayaat of the Glorious Qur'an."
(Tirmidhi, classed as Sahih)

It is also called Al-Hamd and As-Salah because the Prophetﷺ said that his Lord said,

قَسَمْتُ الصَّلَاةَ بَيْنِي وَبَيْنَ عَبْدِي نِصْفَيْنِ، فَإِذَا قَالَ الْعَبْدُ: الْحَمْدُ لِلَّهِ رَبِّ الْعَالَمِينَ، قَالَ اللهُ: حَمِدَنِي عَبْدِي

"The prayer (i.e., Al-Faatiha) is divided into two halves between Me and My servants." When the servant says, "All praise is due to Allah, the Lord of existence," Allah says, "My servant has praised Me."

Al-Faatiha was called the Salaah because reciting it is a condition for the correctness of Salaah - the prayer. Al-Faatiha was also called Ash-Shifaa' (the Cure).

It is also called Ar-Rooqyah (remedy) since, in the Sahih, there is the narration of Abu Sa`id telling the story of the Companion who used Al-Faatiha as a remedy for the tribal chief who was poisoned.

Ibn Jarir said, "The Arabs call every comprehensive matter that contains several specific areas an 'Umm.' For instance, they call the skin that surrounds the brain, Umm Ar-Ra's.

They also call the flag that gathers the ranks of the army an Umm." He also said, "Makkah was called Umm Al-Qura, (the Mother of the Villages) because it is the grandest and the leader of all villages. It was also said that the earth was made starting from Makkah."
(Tafseer Ibn Kathir)

[5] Rasulullahﷺ said that Allah has said, "*I have divided prayer between Myself and My servant into two halves, and My servant shall have what he has asked for. When the servant says: Al-hamdu-lillahi-rabbil-aalamin, Allah says: My servant has praised Me. And when he says: Ar-rahmanir-rahim, Allah (mighty and sublime be He) says: My servant has extolled Me, and when he says: Maliki-yowmiddeen, Allah says: My servant has exalted Me – and on one occasion He said: My servant has submitted to My power. And when he says: Iyyaka-nabudu wa iyyaka-nastaeen, He says: This is between Me and My servant, and My servant shall have what he has asked for. And when he says: Ihdina-siraatal-mustakeem till the end, He says: This is for My servant, and My servant shall have what he has asked for.*"
(Sahih Muslim, Malik, Tirmidhi, Abu Dawood, An-Nisaa'i, and Ibn Majah)

[6] See hadith above.

[7] Allah has said that we should seek refuge with Him from Shaytaan before reciting Qur'aan by

saying, "A-oo-thoo-bill-laa-he-min-nash-shay-taan-nir-ra-jeem."

(So, when you) want to recite the Qur'an, seek refuge with Allah from Shaytaan, the outcast (the cursed one). (Qur'aan 16:98).

The majority of scholars state that reciting this phrase, known as the Isti'aathah in Arabic (pronounced Is-ti-`aa-thah), is recommended and not required, and therefore, not reciting it does not constitute a sin. However, Rasulullah ﷺ always said the Isti`aathah. In addition, the Isti`aathah wards off the evil of Shaytaan, which is necessary; the rule is that the means needed to implement a requirement of the religion is itself also required. And when one says, "I seek refuge with Allah from the cursed devil." Then this will suffice.
(Tafseer Ibn Kathir)

8 Saying the Basmallah, "Bis-mil-laa-hir-rah-maa-nir-ra-heem" before reciting Suratul-Faatiha (or any surah, except for the ninth, Suratut-Towba, which does not have the Basmallah in the beginning) is agreed upon by all scholars past and present.

However, there is some difference of opinion as to whether the Basmallah is part of Suratul-Faatiha (one of its ayaat) or not, and whether or not the Basmallah should be recited aloud in the prayer before reciting Suratul-Faatiha.

We cannot go into a lengthy discussion of this matter here. However, it should be noted that if someone chooses to include the Basmallah as part of Faatiha, there is support for this from the scholars of Islaam (i.e. Imaam Shaaf'i, Abu Hurayrah, and others). If someone chooses not to include the Basmallah as part of the surah, as we have done in this book (the Basmallah is not counted among the seven verses), then there is support for this view as well (i.e. The four Caliphs: Abu Bakr, Umar, Uthmaan, Ali, رضي الله عنهم and scholars such as: Imaan Abu Hanifah, Imaam Ahmed Ibn Hanbal, and others).

The scholars that believe that the Basmallah is part of Suratul-Faatiha, also believe that the Basmallah should be recited aloud in the prayer, based on the fact that it is part of the surah, this is supported by some narrations from the Sahaaba.

Those scholars that do not include the Basmallah as part of the surah, state that the Basmallah should not be said aloud based on the established practice (as recorded in the ahadith) of Rasulullahﷺ and the four Caliphs (leaders of the Muslims) who followed him.

In issues such as these, where there is some difference of opinion, it is best to let children know about the differences, so they will be aware, and not accuse others of doing something wrong. Then make clear to your child which opinion is the one you are most comfortable with and would like him or her to follow, and Allah knows best.

[9] See note #4.

[10] Al-Faatiha is recited in each Rakah of the prayer so if you add all of the Rakaah of the five daily prayers it equals 17. If you add each Rakaah of the Rawaatib Sunnah (these are 12 Sunnah Rakaat that Rasulullahﷺ did before and/or after the daily prayers), then the total is 32. During Ramadaan when Rasulullahﷺ prayed Taraaweeh, or if he added Qiyaamul-Layl and Tahajjood during the night and early morning, he might have recited it many more times in addition to this.

[11] Al-Faatiha was called the Salaah because reciting it is a condition for the correctness of Salaah - the prayer.

[12] The Evil Eye is when a person is affected adversely by the envious look of another person. This envy may be mixed with hate, or it may just be admiration. In either case, it is caused by looking at the object of envy and not praising Allah for the creation of what the person envies or desires.

Many people, even among the Muslims, doubt the existence of the Evil Eye and equate it with superstition. However, the Evil Eye is not a superstition (fear of spirits or harm caused by a deity, jinn, etc.) rather it is harm caused by human beings when they look at something and do not praise Allah for its beauty.

Allah tells us in the Qur'aan to seek protection from the Evil Eye (for example in Suratul-Qalam v. 51, Allah warns Rasulullahﷺ about the Quraysh who wished to affect him by the Evil Eye), and Rasulullahﷺ said, *"The Evil Eye is real!"* (Sahih Al-Bukhari and Sahih Muslim)

13 It (Suratul-Faatiha) is also called Ar-Rooqyah (remedy) since, in the Sahih, there is the narration of Abu Sa`id telling the story of the Companion who used Al-Faatiha as a remedy for the tribal chief who was poisoned. Later, the Messenger of Allahﷺ said to a companion,

وَمَا يُدْرِيكَ أَنَّهَا رُقْيَةٌ

"How did you know that it is a Rooqyah?"

Bibliography

1. Tafseer Ibn Kathir (Abridged), English translation by Shaykh Safiur-Rahman Al-Mubarakpuri, Darussalam Publishers, 2000

2. Sahih Al-Bukhari, English translation by Dr. Muhammed Muhsin Khan, Islamic University, Al-Medina Al-Munawwara, Kazi Publications, 1986

3. Sahih Muslim, English translation by Abdul Hamid Siddiqi, Shaykh Muhammad Ashraf Publishers, 1990

4. The Qur'aan (English translation), Saheeh International, Almunatada Alislami, Abul Qasim Publishing House, 2012

More Products Offered by Ad-Duha!

Ad-Duha is not just a bookstore, we offer complete curriculum packages for use by **homeschoolers or Islamic Schools.**

Our courses contain everything needed to teach in a home or classroom environment including:

- Daily Lesson Manuals
- Full-color, illustrated textbooks (no images of humans/animals)
- Activity filled workbooks
- Audiovisual software (no music or images of humans/animals)
- Enrichment activities for every subject and lesson
- Suggested field trips
- Integrated worksheets to reinforce lesson objectives
- Grading sheets
- Test preparation guides...and much more!

To view samples of all our books and lesson manuals visit our web site at…

www.ad-duha.org

Made in the USA
San Bernardino, CA
20 August 2018